A YEAR OF WEEKLY DEVOTIONALS

FINDING
JOY
in Jesus

Treasures of Truth
to Light Your Heart and Soul

*Keitron)
Delight in the
Lord and He will give
the desires of your
heart! ♡
Psalm 37:4
Jill Lowry*

By Jill Lowry

ISBN- 10: 0-692-05814-1
ISBN-13: 978-0-692-05814-5

Finding Joy in Jesus

Interior photos © 2018 by Jill Lowry
Cover Design by Kerry Prater.
Interior Design by Katharine E. Hamilton

Dedication

Dedicated to my Lord Jesus who gives me abundant joy and everlasting life, my mother who inspired me to write my first book, and my family and friends who have constantly encouraged me to continue pursuing my dreams.

Acknowledgements

This book is dedicated to my loving and giving mother, Julia, who went to be with Jesus on July 4, 2017, after a battle with pancreatic cancer. Her fighting spirit and inner peace throughout the difficult time was evident as she found her joy in Jesus through His word and prayer. She inspired me to keep encouraging others through my scripture photos and writings.

I want to thank my family who has constantly encouraged me to keep sharing the word of God through my photos and writings. Thank you for supporting and loving me.

I would like to thank my praying friends who have prayed consistently and have encouraged me to earnestly pursue the desires of my heart. I enjoy talking about Jesus with you all.

Finally, and most importantly, I give the Lord all the glory and praise for giving me the beautiful images to photograph and the treasures of truth to share with you in the pages of this book. My desire is that you will find the joy of Jesus as you read the words of truth from the Bible. May these words inspire you to grow closer to Jesus!

Contents

Introduction

I am delighted that you are reading "Finding Joy in Jesus." The writings are a compilation of photographs, scriptures, and words that the Lord has given me to share with you so you will find your joy in Jesus!

My desire as you read this book is to encourage and inspire you to find Jesus for the first time or find Him again and be revived and refreshed by the joy that only Jesus gives.

"Finding Joy in Jesus" is my first book. The beginning of my journey for writing this book began when I started taking photographs of the scenes on and around the lake in my hometown in east Texas in 2015. I enjoy the lake so much that I wanted to share these treasures with my friends and family. The Lord kept giving me more beautiful gifts of nature to photograph each day. To thank Him for these gifts, I started sharing my photos by adding a scripture from my daily readings in the Bible. Every day was a new day in the word for me as I created these scripture photos.

The next year as I opened my heart more completely to Him and listened, I heard Him tell me to start writing about each scripture photo. He has given me more gifts in these words from the Holy Spirit. This new way of spending time with Jesus opened up a whole new world for me; a world centered on Jesus where my faith grew deeper and my knowledge of Him and His truth grew stronger in me. My heart and soul were filled with a new joy each day as I began writing for the Lord Jesus!

My desire is to bring the word to others and in doing so, my blessings have doubled because I am able to spend more time with Jesus as I write each day. This double blessing is one that only Jesus can give when we give ourselves to Him completely to be used for His purpose and glory!

My hope is that you will be encouraged and inspired by the words you read and that you will open your heart completely to Jesus and His love for you. In doing so, my prayer is that you will be still and listen to Him calling you to follow the dream that He has placed in your heart.

He has a plan and a future for you. Read His word with fresh eyes and listen with new ears to see and hear the Lord Jesus. Open your heart to His amazing love and grace. You will find your joy in Jesus as you love Him first by spending time with Him each day in His word and in prayer.

I have included some pages in the back of the book for your personal prayers and praises. Use these pages to write your prayers to Jesus. He wants you to spend time with Him in prayer. He bends down to hear you and will answer. Write your praises as Jesus answers you and be encouraged by His love for you.

My prayer is that this book will inspire you to open your Bible and be challenged to spend time reading His treasures of truth. There you will find Jesus when you seek Him. As you seek Him, you will find Him and the desires He has for you. Keep delighting in the Lord and He will give you the desires of your heart!

Find your Joy in Jesus!

Blessings of joy,
Jill Lowry

A YEAR OF WEEKLY DEVOTIONALS

FINDING JOY in Jesus

Treasures of Truth to Light Your Heart and Soul

Find Your Joy in Jesus

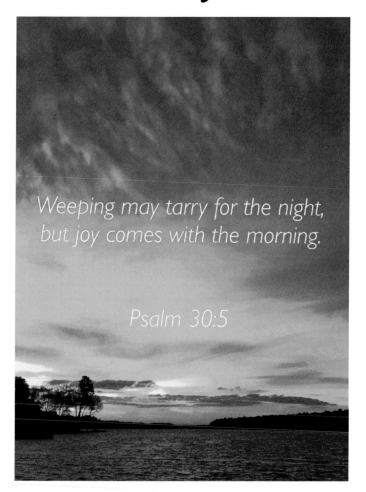

Weeping may tarry for the night,
but joy comes with the morning.

Psalm 30:5

Weeping may tarry for the night, but joy comes in the morning. Yes, joy will come to you when you make the *Lord* first in your life! Seek Him with your whole heart and see how your life will be full of great joy. Only *Jesus* can give you the joy that lasts forever. Find your complete joy in Him. He is waiting to give it to you.

Cast all your cares and anxieties upon the *Lord*. Look to *Jesus* and feel His *Holy Spirit* covering you with protection. Feel the warmth of His love. Call upon Him to save you. He saves you and gives you the freedom you desire. He will mend your broken heart and renew you. Let Him mold you and melt you so that He can use you.

Only *Jesus* can take away your pain and give you peace. He has made you in His image and will create in you a clean heart if you desire. He refreshes you daily so come to Him. Confess your sins to the one who weeps with you and holds your tears in His bottle. Through your tears, you will find joy. With *Jesus*, joy will come. He will make it happen! Just believe!

Strength from the Lord

Finally, be strong in the Lord and in the strength of His might.

Ephesians 6:10

Finally, be strong in the *Lord* and in the strength of His might. He will give you all power and strength when you trust in Him and make *Jesus* the *Lord* of your life. His rays of hope will pour down on you and give you more joy than you ever thought possible. You can have all, when you let Him cover you completely.

Seek first the kingdom of *God* and all good things will be added to you. You will find Him and His eternal treasures in heaven when you search for Him with all of your heart. *Jesus* is right there waiting for you. His mercies are new every morning. His grace has saved you. Stop looking everywhere else for the hope that is in *Jesus*. Your hope is right there beside you waiting for you to receive Him!

Many will look elsewhere for strength and power except to the power of the *Lord*. But those who look to the *Lord* for their strength, will rise up with wings like eagles. They will run and not be weary. They will walk fully clothed in power and faith in the armor of *God*.

Be still and listen. Be ready to go as you are called. Be encouraged by the hope of your calling in *Jesus Christ*. Be strong in the *Lord*, the *God* of all power and glory. He is ready to meet you in the light. Run to Him and be welcomed into your destiny by the *Father of Light*!

With Joy You Will Draw Water from the Wells of Salvation

With joy you will draw water from the wells of salvation.

Isaiah 12:3

With joy you will draw water from the wells of salvation. When you give your heart to *Jesus*, you will have joy that comes from Him. You will know the freedom that comes from salvation. Only the *Lord* can give you this freedom and joy! The joy of *Jesus* will flood your soul and bubble out from inside of you. The freedom you find in *Jesus* will break the chains that bind you because *Jesus* will set you free from your sins! Let *Jesus* be your salvation. His is the living water that you seek. When you seek Him, you will find Him ready and able to give you everything you need. Walk in His love and say yes to making Him the king of your heart.

Your soul needs refreshing from the *Holy Spirit* each day. The power of the *Spirit* will come alive inside of you as you make room for Him. Let *Jesus* fill you with His *Spirit*! Open your eyes to magnificence and wonder from the *Lord*. Open your ears to hear His voice guiding you. Open your heart to receive His love for you. By His stripes you have been healed. By His wounds you have been made new. By His death and resurrection, you have been saved. *Jesus* gives you living water. Draw from His living waters of salvation and find joy everlasting!

God's Work in You

For it is God who works in you,
both to will and to work for his good pleasure.

Philippians 2:13

For it is *God* who works in you, both to will and to work for His good pleasure. Praise the *Lord* who gives you this opportunity to work for Him and with Him. He loves seeing your heart connect with others as you serve. He watches with joy as you tell the good news about Him and His love. He sees the light shining in you as you spread the gospel truth. Go tell it on the mountain. Tell of your hope that is in *Christ Jesus*. Give the love that you receive so generously from your *Savior*.

Bask in His glory and His gift of great grace. Praise your *Lord* for giving you *Jesus*!

His holiness and righteousness are alive and active in you as you activate the *Holy Spirit* inside you. Your life will be blessed with His favor as you make the *Lord* first in your life and follow Him where He is calling you. He lives in you and wants to bless you abundantly.

Let Him bless you and keep you. Let Him cover you with His mercy that is never ending. Let Him work in you so that His will can be done through and in you. Let *Jesus* in, and you will never be the same again! *Jesus* will heal your body, soul, and mind completely and make you whole again! Amen!

Lean on Christ

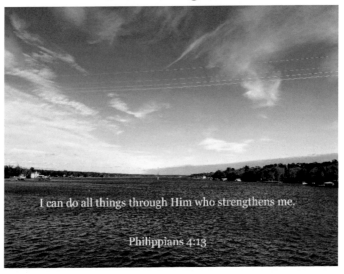

I can do all things through Him who strengthens me.

Philippians 4:13

You can do all things through Him who strengthens you. *Jesus* helps you and will give you strength when you are weak. He is your strong tower and your refuge. Seek *Jesus* and you will find Him. Ask and you shall receive. Knock and the door to life will be opened for you. He is waiting to give you more peace and joy. Ask *Jesus* for more, and you will receive more.

Jesus is your fountain of life and your well spring of joy. He is waiting for you to come to Him so He can bless you and fill you with more. Get to know your *Savior* by trusting Him and letting Him guide you into all truth. He is the way to life everlasting. When you give Him control of your life, He will direct your path and keep you close to Him. Only *Jesus* can fulfill all of His promises to you. He will never fail you. He will never let you down. Believe, and you will receive all that He has for you. Only good and perfect things come down to you from your *Lord*! Bask in the joy of *Jesus* and the hope of His calling for you. *Jesus* is the peace you need. Lean on Him and His love will comfort and encourage you.

Only *Jesus* can be there right when you need Him. Call upon Him and do not fear because *Jesus* is near. You can do all things through *Jesus Christ* who strengthens you! Do you believe? Will you call upon Him? Believe, and you will be blessed, loved, and strengthened beyond measure! Amen!

Walk in Righteousness
with the Lord

For the Lord knows the way
of the righteous,
but the way of the wicked
will perish.

Psalm 1:6

For the *Lord* knows the way of the righteous, but the way of the wicked will perish. The *Lord* knows your heart. He knows your intentions and your desires. He wants you to walk in the path of righteousness with Him. Those who walk faithfully on the path with Him, will find life. And those who walk in the way of evil, will perish.

You are free to decide which way you will live. If you stay connected to the *Lord* and walk with Him, you will be forever changed and renewed. If you walk without the *Lord*, your life will be empty and dead. The *Lord* rewards the pure in heart, for they shall see Him. The *Lord* seeks the pure in *Spirit*, for they shall know Him.

The *Lord* loves you abundantly and generously. He forgives and redeems you from your sins. It is never too late to come to the *Lord*. He saves you with His amazing grace. He washes away your sins and gives you mercy. Turn away from your sins, and turn your heart toward His Son, *Jesus*. He died for you so that you would be free to live and to love! The only way to freedom is through *Jesus Christ*!

Taste and see that *Jesus* is good. Make Him the *Lord* of your life. Put Him first, and you will feel the rays of hope shining brightly on you, warming every part of your body and soul. With *Jesus*, your heart will glow with a fire that will burn eternally!

See the Majesty and
Glory of the Lord

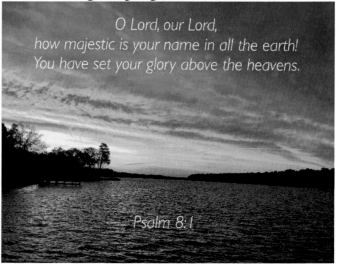

O Lord, our Lord,
how majestic is your name in all the earth!
You have set your glory above the heavens.

Psalm 8:1

O *Lord*, our *Lord*, how majestic is your name in all the earth! You have set your glory above the heavens. You have shown us your glory! You are mighty indeed, and there is no way that we can look at the wonder and beauty of what you create and not see your power!

You have given us a new gift every morning if we will just open our eyes to see. There is much joy waiting for us to behold. You give us mercy and grace just when we need it. You, *Lord*, are so good to us. We want to have more of you and less of us.

Help us to look to you for help and take your hand. Your outstretched arms reach out to us from the heavens. You reach for us with your strong arms, so that we can take hold of your hand. You promise to hold us up and never let go!

Your glorious light shines down on us, and your rays touch us with your power. You are mighty to save and all powerful! We are drawn to you and your saving grace. Only your grace can save us! Only your power can infuse us with life everlasting! We believe! We are freed!

Rejoice in the Lord with a Thankful Heart

Therefore my heart is glad, and my whole being rejoices; my flesh also dwells secure.

Psalm 16:9

Therefore, our heart is glad, and our whole being rejoices; our flesh also dwells secure. We know that you, *Lord*, are the reason we have peace and security. We praise you for giving us your right hand to help hold us up. We magnify your name for always loving us. You comfort us and our whole being rests securely in your powerful love!

Our souls are being renewed each day because of you. We feel your exuberant joy flooding our hearts and your peace settling in our souls. Only you can make us whole again.

We praise you for your mercy and love. We are thankful and give you all the glory and honor for being ever present for us. You never fail us, *Lord*! With thankful hearts we praise your *Holy* name! Our hearts rejoice as we sing our songs of thanksgiving to you, *Lord*!

Our blessings are bountiful, because you have given us many. We will focus on you and not our concerns. When we put our whole being in your hands, we find freedom that only you can give us. We find the lasting joy that only comes from you, *Lord*. We experience real hope and true peace that is ours in you.

We know that we will find everything we need in you, *Lord*. We have a thankful spirit stuffed with your grace. We will give grace as we have received it in abundance. We will trust in you, *Lord*, to do more. You can, and will, do more through us, and for us, than we could ever dream or imagine! Our praise will ever be on our lips as we sing to you with grateful hearts! We are thankful for you, *Lord*! Amen!

Let the Lord Rescue You

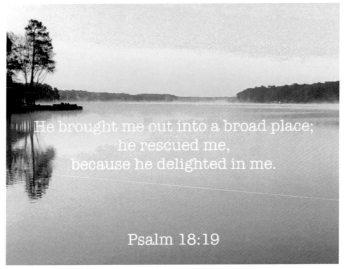

He brought me out into a broad place;
he rescued me,
because he delighted in me.

Psalm 18:19

He brought you out into a broad place; he rescued you, because he delighted in you. The *Lord* sees your struggles and He knows your pain. He will rescue you if you let Him. He delights in you and wants your whole heart. Come to Him and make the *Lord* your refuge.

Take shelter in His wings and find hope in His love. He needs you to be ready in and out of season to share the hope that He gives you. His hope is real hope. Do not be afraid to surrender all to Him. He is waiting for you to come and find comfort and rest in Him. Abandon self for more of *God* in your life. You can be sure of His everlasting love for you. You are safe in His strong arms. You will find rest for your weary body and food for your hungry soul. Only the *Lord* can give you complete peace. His place of peace is the perfect place to live each day.

Come to life with the *Lord* and you will never walk alone. You will sing a new song of joy and be energized with His great grace upon you. He loves you and wants you. Delight in the *Lord*, and He will give you the desires of your heart!

Encourage and Build Others Up

Therefore, encourage one another and build
one another up,
just as you are doing

1 Thessalonians 5:11

Therefore, encourage one another and build one another up, just as you are doing. *God* rejoices when He sees His children coming together. He loves when you encourage others by meeting needs in their lives. *God* wants you to love and live together in harmony and peace.

You can make a difference by choosing to give and to serve others. *God* loves a cheerful giver. He cherishes the gifts given from the heart. Your special gift of encouragement will bless and build others up so that they can see *Jesus* in you. Be that encourager and you will bless others and receive the blessing that comes from giving. There are people waiting for you to lift their spirits. Find those people and bless them. Seek others before yourself and meet needs in their lives. You might be that one person who can bring them closer to *God*. Yes, that person could be you.

Start today by asking *God* to give you the desire to help others. Start meeting needs and lifting spirits and you will find treasures in heaven. There is exuberant joy in serving others! There is eternal hope in encouraging others! There is everlasting peace in comforting others! You will find that joy, hope, and peace as you shine your light on someone in need. Shine on!

Believe that Everything
is Possible

Everything is possible
for him who believes.

Mark 9:23

Jesus tells us that everything is possible to those that believe. He does not say some things are possible, but everything is possible. We must have faith and keep our eyes fixed on *Jesus*, the author and perfecter of our faith. He will answer us if we come to Him believing that He can and will provide for our every need. He will restore our hearts and renew our minds when we keep seeking Him.

As we surrender to the *Lord*, His rays of glory will give us new strength and power from the *Holy Spirit*. The *Spirit* inside us will give us hope and direct our paths through the dark wilderness of lost hope.

We will see miracles in our lives. When the world has given up, we must continue praying in belief that what we hope for will come to pass. We believe, because we worship a powerful *God* who we know can do all things. He promises good to those who trust in Him and love Him with all their heart.

Seek His will above all else and follow His light. Keep praying big, trusting big, and believing big, for our *God* is big. He can do the impossible, and He will never give up on you. The *Lord* is patiently waiting for you to believe! What are you waiting for?

Let the Good Shepherd Lead You

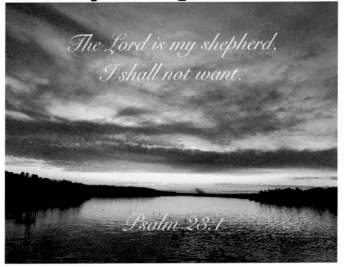

The Lord is my shepherd,
I shall not want.

Psalm 23:1

The *Lord* is our shepherd. We shall not want. He gives us exactly what we need and clothes us with mercy and grace. He revives us and makes us whole again. We are never wanting when we are His. We have everything we need in the *Lord*. He is enough!

His power and strength overwhelm and overpower us to do more than we ever thought possible. He gives us rest when we are weary and strength to do what He needs us to do. We are alive in Him as He gives us new life each day. He takes our thoughts and our dreams and makes them bigger and better than we could have ever imagined. All we have to do is trust, obey, and believe our *Good Shepherd*. He will lead us if we will follow.

When we ask and believe we will receive, He gives even more abundantly. Only the *Lord* knows what we need and how everything will work together for good. Let us trust Him to meet our needs and the desires of our hearts. We are rewarded with more blessings when we give generously from the heart. Be blessed by blessing others. Dream big and pray bigger for our *Lord* will surely do it!

Let the Lord Direct Your Hearts to the Love of God

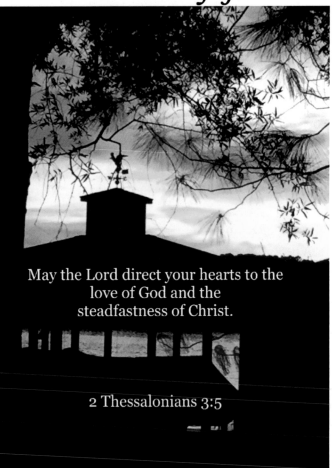

May the Lord direct your hearts to the love of God and the steadfastness of Christ.

2 Thessalonians 3:5

May the *Lord* direct your hearts to the love of *God* and the steadfastness of *Christ*. When your heart is directed to the *Lord*, you will be able to feel His love and know the power of His mighty hand. He is the one who will lead you into all truth, but you are the one who must follow where He leads you. You must press on with the *Lord* as He directs your path.

Christ will give you the ability to walk steadfastly and run swiftly. You will rise with wings like eagles as you let go and put your full trust in *Jesus*. He will never let you fall when He is holding you up. His will for you is to be with Him. He is waiting for you to join your heart with His.

Do not fear because the *Lord* is near. He will protect you from evil and will guard your heart if you let Him. Keep asking in faith, and you will receive. Keep believing, and you will find. Keep knocking, and the door you are searching for will be opened to you.

Jesus has overcome the world for you. He is ready to embrace you with His loving arms. He is eager to show you the way to peace through trusting Him. When you seek Him and His will, you will find hope. Through this peace and hope, you will find joy! Find your peace, hope, and joy in the love of *Jesus*!

Stand By the Lord and He Will Strengthen You

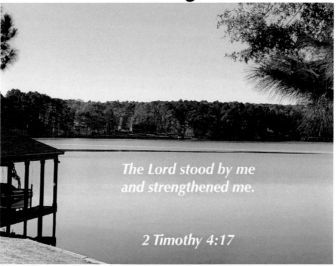

The Lord stood by me and strengthened me.

2 Timothy 4:17

The *Lord* will stand by you and strengthen you. He gives you what you need if you will just ask Him. He loves you and will help you. Draw onto Him and seek Him with your whole heart. Do not be afraid or anxious, for the *Lord* will surely do it!

He will provide all for you, His beloved. He wants you to live joyfully with hope in your heart. Only *Jesus* can give you a life filled with pure joy if you so desire. Come to *Jesus* and come to Life! Through *Jesus*, you will find the life you have been searching for. You will be blessed beyond measure with *Jesus* when you say yes to Him!

Jesus Christ came to give you life everlasting. He is your overcomer, so trust in Him to rescue you from that pit. Let your faith be bigger than your fears. Let your joy be big because your *Lord* is bigger! He can do what is impossible for man. Only through *Jesus* can you be saved! Trust in Him and you will see your dreams come alive through *Jesus Christ*! Find your joy in *Jesus*!

Walk By Faith

According to your faith be it done to you.

Matthew 9:29

According to your faith be it done to you. *Jesus* performed many miracles for the faithful. He gave sight to the blind, healed the sick, and raised the dead as they believed. Their faith was great, and *Jesus* recognized and rewarded this faith. Do you believe? Is your faith strong and alive now? Are you ready to receive blessings and see miracles?

Jesus promises eternal rewards to those who believe. When you pray in His name, He intercedes to the *Father* on your behalf. He wants to bless you greatly. He yearns to have a deeper relationship with you. He needs you to faithfully work for Him. *God* created us with the desire to work for Him. Ask Him what He desires for you and do it! You are His hands and feet who He needs on earth to accomplish much for the kingdom. There is much work to do for the *Lord*. You can be that person who will make a difference in the lives of many. Loving others well will bring a double blessing of joy!

Seek the *Lord*, and He will show you how you can meet a need in someone's life. There are many needs and not enough willing people to meet those needs. Stand up, and faithfully go where you know *God* is calling you. Be the blessing you were created to be for *Christ*. Your faith will be rewarded, and your heart will be revived as you walk by faith!

Fight the Good Fight of Faith

Fight the good fight of the faith.

1 Timothy 6:12

Fight the good fight of the faith. The *Lord* knows your heart and loves your faith. Your faith will restore you to a place of hope. Your hope will bring you to a place a peace. Your perfect peace from the *Lord* will give you pure joy. Keep fighting the good fight and your faith will grow stronger.

Be still and know that He is *God*. Listen to Him calling you out to find Him through your faith. He has designed a plan for you. You may not see all the details, but He is there with you. Follow Him to find life. He is your spring of life! He is your river of peace and your fountain of joy!

Only the *Lord* can give you everything you need. He is the one who will restore your heart and your soul. He renews you day by day when you believe!

Ask *Jesus* to give you more of Him. Yes, more of *Jesus*! Your faith will come alive as *Jesus* grows deeper inside of you. Your heart that was once hard and brittle by the struggles of the world, will soften and beat stronger through your faith in *Christ*. Keep fighting the good fight of the faith with *Jesus* by your side! He is well pleased with you, faithful one!

Magnify and Exalt the Lord

Oh, magnify the Lord with me,
and let us exalt his name together!

Psalm 34:3

Oh, magnify the *Lord* with us, and let us exalt His name together! For our *Lord* is almighty and all powerful. There is nothing that He cannot do! He will show us miracles and answer prayers for us in mighty ways! Believe that He can and will do the impossible!

Our *Lord* wants to pour His blessings upon us. His greatest desire is to have a deeper relationship with all of His children. He longs to know us more. He wants us to serve Him faithfully and pursue Him passionately. Let us pour our hearts out to the *Lord* and magnify Him! Only the *Lord* can heal us. He is the one who mends broken hearts and softens hearts of stone. His powerful love will restore and revive us again! Let us come back to the *Savior* and rest in His arms once again.

Let us exalt His name with fellow believers and feel His presence invigorate our souls. Let us lift our voices and praise His Holy name together! There is power in the name of *Jesus*, our *Lord*! Magnify Him!

Seek the Lord's Face

You have said, "Seek my face."
My heart says to you,
"Your face, Lord, do I seek."

Psalm 27:8

The *Lord* is well pleased when we seek His face and look to Him. He loves us so much and has much to show us. As He speaks to us, let us listen with anticipation and gladness. Let us hear His words of hope and truth that He gives us. Let us go where He sends us. Let us open our heart to His overpowering love for us. Only the *Lord* can cover us with abundant joy and peace as we seek Him. When we believe with our hearts and confess with our mouths that His *Son Jesus* is *Lord*, the glory of the *Lord* shines upon us and we are free to live victoriously through *Christ our Savior*!

We do not have to walk down that path alone. We have *Jesus* with us. He is for us and meets our every need. We once were lost without Him, but now are found as we open our hearts to His love. We were once weak, but now have strength through *Jesus* who gives us renewed strength. Go seek the *Lord Jesus*. He wants us to show Him our face. He needs us to give Him our whole heart. He desires the best for us. He yearns for us to say yes to Him!

Say yes to the one who will save us! Keep believing and see how the *Lord* will do the impossible! Our dreams will be bigger and better than we ever thought possible when the *Lord* is our anchor. Be anchored by faith and find His magnificent joy, peace, and hope by saying yes to *Jesus Christ*!

See the Heavens that Declare the Glory of the Lord

You, Lord, laid the foundation of the earth in the beginning, and the heavens are the work of your hands.

Hebrews 1:10

You, *Lord*, laid the foundation of the earth in the beginning, and the heavens are the work of your hands. Yes, *Lord*, you made the heavens and the earth and all that is within. We are thankful for your signs of wonder to us each day. We praise you for showing us each masterpiece that you paint in the heavens! The heavens declare your glory!

We see what you want us to see, because we are looking for you. You captivate us with your magnificence, and we look in awe every time we see a new sign in the sky. Thank you for showing us your love each time you paint a new picture. We see hope in the clouds, joy in the sunrise, and peace in the sunset. Your rays of joy send warm hugs to us. Your sprinkles of rain cleanse and refresh us. Your rainbows of hope renew our spirit. We have peace once again, as we see your signs and know that you have saved us from our sins because of your love for us.

You even paint crosses in the heavens to remind us that you love us so much that you gave us your only *Son*, *Jesus* so that we may have salvation. Yes, you sacrificed all so that we may live! We praise you, and love you so much, *Lord*! Our hearts are full of wonder and thanksgiving! We cling to your promises and will trust in you always and forever! Amen!

Drawing Nearer to God by Faith

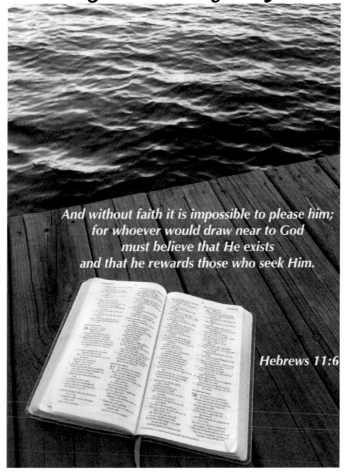

And without faith it is impossible to please him;
for whoever would draw near to God
must believe that He exists
and that he rewards those who seek Him.

Hebrews 11:6

And without faith it is impossible to please Him, for whoever would draw near to *God* must believe that He exists and that He rewards those who seek Him. We need to keep believing and drawing nearer to *God*. He wants us to believe. He rewards our faithful actions. He desires our hearts to be connected by faith.

Joy will be ours when we keep believing and drawing closer to our *Father*. We will feel free when we let go and let *God* take over our life. He wants to do what is best for us. He needs us to give Him our whole heart so that He can do a new work inside of us.

The *Lord* will make us new if we let Him take over and surrender all to Him. More joy will be ours as we surrender more to Him. Let us be still and know that He is *God*. Say yes to all that He is wanting to give. Believe that He is ready to bless our lives with greater joy! Taste and see that the *Lord* is so good. Please the *Lord* by drawing closer to Him by faith. He rewards those who seek Him first. Blessings are waiting for the faithful ones! Be one of His faithful followers and be filled with abundant joy!

Look to Jesus, the Founder and Perfecter of Our Faith

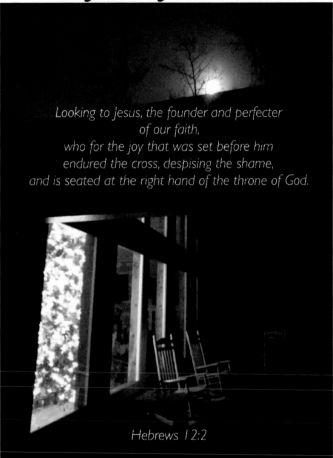

Looking to Jesus, the founder and perfecter
of our faith,
who for the joy that was set before him
endured the cross, despising the shame,
and is seated at the right hand of the throne of God.

Hebrews 12:2

Looking to *Jesus*, the founder and perfecter of our faith, who for the joy that was set before Him endured the cross, despising the shame, and is seated at the right hand of the throne of *God*. Let *Jesus* be the song of your heart. He suffered on the cross for you so that you would have joy everlasting. Only *Jesus* can give you this joy! He is the author of your faith through His life and resurrection. Draw to Him and believe that He loves you dear one. You are His beloved child whom He adores. Give Him your sins and your shame and believe that He will wash them away. You are forgiven and free with *Jesus Christ*! Only *Jesus* can give you life!

He has much to give you if you will simply take all that is yours in *Christ Jesus*. There is hope waiting for you behind all your pain and suffering. There is peace for you when you follow *Jesus* by faith where He leads you. There is joy for you when you obey Him and reciprocate His love by trusting Him completely. There is love for you when you accept your gift of salvation.

Take your hope, peace, joy and love that comes from a relationship with *Jesus Christ*! You will experience a new life infused with the *Spirit* of the living *God*! Your heart and soul will be full! It's your choice and your life. It's time to magnify the *Lord* and say yes!

Know that Jesus Christ is the Same Yesterday, Today, and Forever

Jesus Christ is the same yesterday and today and forever.

Hebrews 13:8

Jesus Christ is the same yesterday and today and forever. He is never changing and constant. His love for you is steady and sure. *Jesus* will never leave or fail you. Draw to Him and let Him be the joy in your heart! Anticipate His new blessings for you each day by leaning into Him more.

Thirst for His joy that will fill your heart! Let His love conquer all in your life. When He is first in your life, your days will be filled with the light of His love. Your nights will be filled with His peace as you find rest for your body and soul. Eagerly receive the love He is waiting to give you.

Be still in His presence and know that He is your *Lord* and *Savior*. Wait with longing for what the *Lord* wants to give you. Bask in the glory He will show you! Be steady and strong. Be faithful and true to your *Lord*. He wants to see your face. Show Him your face and come to Him!

Only *Jesus* can give you all that you need. He will surely do it! Ask and you shall receive. Seek and you shall find. Pray without ceasing and you will find the answers you seek. The *Lord* bends down to listen, and He longs to give you the desires of your heart. Trust Him with your whole heart and discover that He is all that you need! Only *Jesus* is the same yesterday today and forever! Amen!

You are Justified by Works and Not Faith Alone

You see that a person is justified by works and not faith alone.

James 2:24

You see that a person is justified by works and not faith alone. Yes, faith coupled with works is how *Jesus* wants us to live. He is well pleased when we live out what we believe. We are justified when our faith brings about good works for *Jesus*.

Pray, be active with other believers, give and serve faithfully. See to it that you are living your life following *Jesus* and the purpose to which you have been called. Rest in His presence and feel His love flowing through you and out to others in need. Host the power and presence of the *Holy Spirit* in your life. Find freedom and life through *Jesus* who is life! Choose *Jesus* and choose life.

He wants to give life everlasting and peace beyond understanding. He is your joy right now on earth and will remain your joy someday in heaven. Until that day, find your joy in Him today and forever by honoring Him through your faith and your works. He loves your faithful heart and your serving hands and feet. He sees you helping others by humbly serving where you are called. Go, be *Jesus* to someone today. It is more blessed to give than to receive!

Humble Yourselves Before the Lord

Humble yourselves before the Lord,
and he will exalt you.

James 4:10

Humble yourselves before the *Lord*, and He will exalt you. Let humility be present in your life. Let go of all pride and selfishness. Put the *Lord* first in your life so that He can exalt you. His presence will overwhelm you with joy if you seek Him first!

The *Lord* is your shepherd. When you let Him lead you, you will not want. He will give you all you need. He will protect you and guide you. The *Lord* will overshadow you with His *Holy Spirit* if you seek His covering and presence. Only the humble will receive all that is theirs in *Christ*.

Turn aside from your selfish ways and turn towards *Christ* so that He can change your heart. He sees your heart and knows your every thought. He desires good for you and His plans are to give you a future and a hope. You must choose this path of freedom and wholeness with *Christ*. Let go of all the barriers to this freedom with Him. Work out your salvation by trusting the *Lord* with every part of your heart, mind, and soul! Believe that you can have this life of joy in *Christ*! Your joy will be complete when you lay aside your pride and come to the foot of the cross with *Jesus*!

Look upon the Lord in His Sanctuary and Behold His Power and Glory

So I have looked upon you in the sanctuary,
beholding your power and glory.

Psalm 63:2

So, we have looked upon you in the sanctuary, beholding your power and glory. Your power is amazing, and your glory is everlasting! We are overwhelmed by you, *Lord Jesus*! We believe that you are going to show us more than we ever thought possible. Our faith will be our eyes sooner than we can ever imagine. You have saved us so that we could experience true freedom and joy. You have given us your *Holy Spirit* so that we can feel your presence and guidance all the time. You have loved us deeply so that we can experience life now and forevermore!

We are freed because you have loved us unconditionally and abundantly. We never have to wonder about your love, but instead can experience the wonder of your love! Your love is true. Your love is real. Your love never ends. Your love saves. Your love brings hope, peace, and joy! Your love is what we all need!

Let us draw nearer to you *Lord* and your overpowering love each day and give you our very best yes. We are better when we are full of your love and are able to give your love to others. Our faith will bring us closer to you. We may not see all the details of our journey, but we will dare to hope by trusting and loving you first! We surrender all to you *Lord*, because you have surrendered all to us first!

Keep Praying and God will Listen and Attend to the Voice of Your Prayer

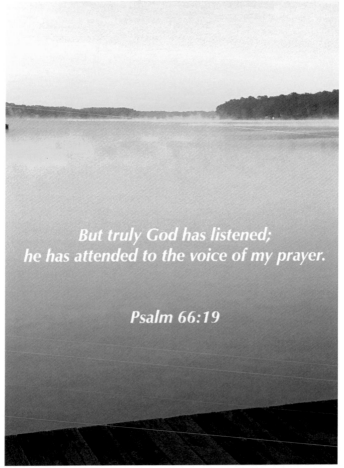

But truly God has listened;
he has attended to the voice of my prayer.

Psalm 66:19

But truly *God* has listened; He has attended to the voice of your prayer. *God* wants you to pray. He hears your prayers and He answers your prayers. Know that He desires for you to call upon Him and pray so that He can know the desires of your heart. The *Lord* wants a deeper relationship with you and that happens when you meet Him through prayer.

God meets you as you call to Him. He bends down to listen to you. He has attended to your voice and knows the sound of your voice. He will surely answer you if you choose to call upon Him. Do not be afraid to ask what your heart desires. If it is the will of *God*, He will answer the desires of your heart. When you continue seeking Him, your desires will be His.

He knows and wants what is best for you, so His answer may be even better than what you have requested. You might have to wait longer to get that answer or it might never be answered exactly how you thought, but the *Lord* hears you and always answers!

Call upon the *Lord* and pray without ceasing. The earnest prayers of a righteous person have great power and are working! Come to the cross and find all the answers to your prayers. All you need is *Jesus*. The *Lord* is your righteousness. You can have a right relationship with *God* through His *Son Jesus*. Your greatest desire to have life, joy, peace, hope, and love are found at the foot of the cross. Meet your *Savior* there and believe!

Following Jesus

If anyone would come after me,
let him deny himself and take up his cross and follow me.

Matthew 16:24

If anyone would come after *Jesus*, let him deny himself and take up His cross and follow *Jesus*. We are each made by *Jesus*, for Him, so that He can use us. In order to follow Him, we must deny ourselves by giving Him control of our lives. Surrendering all to *Jesus*, our blessed *Savior*, is the way to find Him.

When we find Him, let us not let go of Him. He needs to fill us full with His love! He wants us to know Him more deeply. He wants us to serve Him more passionately. He yearns for us to follow Him completely by surrendering all. When we do, we will experience more joy than we ever thought possible. We will have a peace that we cannot explain except that it is given to us by *Jesus*.

Follow Him and find the blessings through the hardships of life. Our struggles will turn around, and we will see joy in the trials. The joy of the *Lord* will be our strength! The hope we have tried to find through the world will be seen through the eyes of *Jesus*. He takes the scales off of our eyes so that we can see. We see what we once could not see.

When we find *Jesus,* and take up His cross and follow Him, our lives will be blessed beyond measure with the power of His *Spirit*. Let us find and follow *Jesus Christ* today! Today is the day that the *Lord* has made for us to live alive and connected to Him. Let us rejoice and be glad in it!

Let Your Soul Thirst for the Living God

My soul thirsts for God,
for the living God.

Psalm 42:2

Your soul thirsts for *God*, for the living *God*. Only *God* can fully satisfy the thirst of your soul and the desires of your heart. Let Him fill you as you drink of His living water that refreshes and brings life. He wants to bring you water that satisfies. He yearns to see you born again with His everlasting life. Let Him fill you completely with His water so that you will never thirst again!

Come to *Jesus*, and you will be free from the chains that bind you. Let His *Spirit* fill you completely. Let His love comfort you.

As you let the *Lord* work in you, your life will be made whole, and you will be able to feel His love transform your heart and soul. *Jesus* lives in you to transform you in His image. He yearns to see you come alive. He works within you so that you will be able to be His hands and feet here on earth. He needs you to come to Him ready and eager to work so that others may be blessed by knowing the truth. The truth will set us free! Keep spreading the truth found in *God's* word that brings life.

The fields are white and ready to be harvested by you. There is much work to be done for *God's* kingdom. See the needs around you and go where you are called. The time is now! There is joy to be harvested! There is hope to be found in the living water of *Jesus*! You will never thirst again when you have *Jesus*!

Ask in the Name of Jesus and You Shall Receive

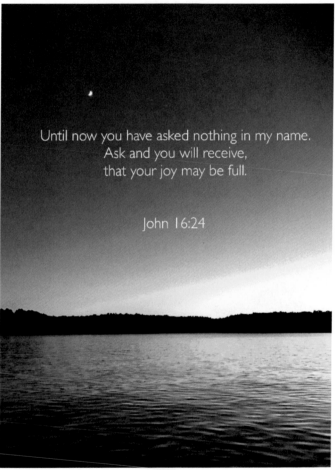

Until now you have asked nothing in my name.
Ask and you will receive,
that your joy may be full.

John 16:24

Jesus said, "Until now you have asked nothing in my name. Ask and you will receive, that your joy may be full." *Jesus* wants us to pray in His name so that we can receive what He wills for us. He wants us to call to Him so that He can give us the desires of our heart as He wishes. He wants good for us and waits patiently for us to come to Him with our requests. *Jesus* does answer us. He will intercede for us to the *Father* as we pray in His name.

Let us believe that we will receive, so that our joy may be full! *Jesus* wants what is best for us and knows that we will find joy when we trust in Him. He wants to know us more intimately, as He loves us so deeply! His love is amazing and real. His grace and mercy never end. It is new every morning!

Find hope in *Jesus Christ*! He will cover us completely with His hope as we surrender all to Him. He will make all things new again for us. Never again will we doubt when we are fully connected to *Jesus*. Ask in His name to receive all that is yours in *Jesus Christ*!

You will be Called Oaks of Righteousness

They may be called oaks of righteousness,
the planting of the Lord,
that He may be glorified.

Psalm 61:3

They may be called oaks of righteousness, the planting of the *Lord*, that He may be glorified, just as we are planted by the *Lord* to minister to those around us. He plants us and gives us what we need to grow strong roots so that we can spread His love. His love is the first fruit He gives us, so that we may grow stronger with deeper roots. As we receive this love, we grow courage and are able to endure much. We find joy even in the hard times of our life because we are grounded in faith. Our peace grows as our roots grow deeper in the *Lord*! Then, we are able to be patient and kind towards those around us who are watching us.

Our goodness and gentleness come out in our actions of faithful service even in the hardest of conditions. We delight in the *Lord* and the desires of our heart are in sync with the *Lord*. We live a life of joy, because of our love for the *Lord*. We are able to be self-controlled. We want more of what *God* wants for us. These are the fruits of the *Spirit* that the *Lord* wants to grow in us. We must first receive all that He wants to give us to thrive on this land. There will be sunshine, misting rain, and rainbows. But there will also be storm clouds, thunder, and lightning. We must receive *Jesus* to stay the course with *Jesus* in the good times and the bad times. Let us not be afraid or discouraged by what is in front of us.

Let us cling to the *Lord* and let Him plant us where He desires. Only then will we be able to see the beauty all around us with our eyes of *Jesus*. His compassion will become reality and His burden will become ours. Only then will we be able to minister to those around us lacking their strong roots in the *Lord*! The oaks around us will not thrive if we ignore our calling from the *Lord* to help them. We can all do our part to nourish them by our love. Let us be filled with the love of the *Lord* and go where we are called. It's time to go!

Finding Hope and Joy Continually in the Lord

But I will hope continually
and will praise you yet more and more.

Psalm 71:14

But we will hope continually and will praise you more and more. We will find our hope and joy in you *Lord*. You have always been there for us and have never let us down. Every day we will be filled with joy, because we have chosen you over ourselves. We have dared to hope, because we have decided to love and follow you first. Our whole heart is yours, *Lord*.

You are the solid rock on which we stand. All other ground is unstable and moveable, but you *Lord* are immovable and steady. We are securely planted in you. We plant our feet in the soil of your love so that we may grow stronger each day. The roots you grow in us are deep, because we are planted with hope and strengthened with your living water. We want more of you and less of ourselves. We lean on you and know that you will never fail us. We need your guidance and wise counsel as we press onward with the work that you have given us.

The harvest is plentiful, but the laborers are few. We want to be one of your faithful laborers. You have called us to love others around us. We will seek your will and your way, *Lord*. We will go serve as you have called us. We will walk faithfully with you where you lead us. You make our path straight, and we will walk in it with joy and praise you more and more!

Seek the Holy and Great Way of Our God

Your way, O God, is holy.
What god is great like our God?

Psalm 77:13

Your way, *O God*, is holy. What god is great like our *God*? Yes, you are our holy and mighty *God*! Nothing is too hard for you! You have made the heavens and the earth and all that is within it! You have placed the stars in the sky to provide us a million lights of hope. You have given us rays of sunshine to light our path. You have lit a fire within us that has renewed our heart and stirred our soul eternally.

Lord, your glory reigns true and speaks to our heart. We are made complete in you, *Lord*. We thank you and love you for always being there for us. We need more of you in our lives. Fill us with a fresh encounter of your *Holy Spirit* each day so that we can be free in you. We feel your mighty power in our lives when we cling to you. Only you can give us all that we need. You are so good to us all the time. We need more of you and less of us!

Help us to lay aside our selfish ways and let you have control! We are ready to be blessed! Blessed is the one who lets His heart be transformed by your glory. We want to be one of your faithful servants who has been revived and made new. Help us to be ready and willing to be all that we can be for you. Your love overwhelms and encourages us because we see your wonders and miracles through our faith in you! Thank you for being ever present in our lives because we have chosen you, *Lord*, the best portion!

Be Firm in Your Faith

If you are not firm in your faith,
you will not be firm at all.

Isaiah 7:9

If you are not firm in your faith, you will not be firm at all. Stay firm and sure of your faith in your *Lord Jesus* He will surely do it! You may not see all the details, but the *Lord Jesus* is working all things for your good. Believe what you hope for and keep trusting in your *Lord* and *Savior* faithfully.

Is your faith faltering or steady? *Jesus* is always faithful to you! So, trust in Him with all of your heart and lean not on your own understanding. Acknowledge Him in all of your ways and He will make your path straight. On the path with your *Lord Jesus* is the best place to be. He will always be there. Believe that you are never alone!

He is the light in your darkest days. He is your hope when all seems hopeless. He is your peace when things seem to be falling apart all around you. He is your joy when you give Him your whole heart. Yes, your joy will be complete in Him. You will find everything you need in *Jesus*! Trust Him and obey Him to stay firm in your faith. Stand up for His truth. Stand firm for your faith in *Jesus Christ*!

Let the Lord God be Your Sun and Shield so that He can Bestow Favor and Honor to You

For the Lord God is a sun and a shield;
the Lord bestows favor and honor.
No good thing does he withhold
from those who walk uprightly.

Psalm 84:11

For the *Lord God* is a sun and a shield. The *Lord* bestows favor and honor. No good thing does He withhold from those who walk uprightly. Yes, the *Lord* does good for those who love Him and obey His commands. He loves us so much that He protects us from evil and keeps us safe from harm. He warms our hearts and nourishes our souls with His great love. We do not need to be afraid when we put our trust in the *Lord*. He bestows favor and honor to His faithful ones. He gives us the desires of our hearts when we delight in Him and His ways. He promises good and will work out all things for us, if we just believe.

Never stop believing and never stop loving our *Lord*. Our help comes from Him! Are we trusting Him wholeheartedly with great faith? Are we believing that the *Lord* can and will answer our prayers? Are we humbly and boldly coming before His throne? Let us trust, obey, believe, and come to the *Lord* with humble hearts so that He can bless us with His favor and honor. He is our sun and our shield. The *Lord* is our hope and our joy. Seek the *Lord* and you will find Him. Be still and know that He is *God*. Spend time with the *Lord* by drawing into Him more. It is time to give it all to the one who gave all to us!

God is Our Salvation

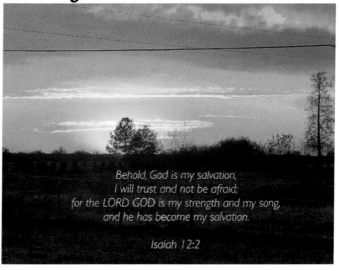

Behold, God is my salvation,
I will trust and not be afraid;
for the LORD GOD is my strength and my song,
and he has become my salvation.

Isaiah 12:2

Behold, *God* is our salvation, we will trust and not be afraid. For the *Lord God* is our strength and our song, and He has become our salvation. Our salvation rests in *God*. Let us know and believe this truth. Because of this gift of salvation, we can move mountains together. We are free and alive with the power of the *Holy Spirit* living inside of us.

Without *God*, we will fail. With *God*, we have increased strength and power that He gives to those who believe. Let us sing His praises forever! Let us feel His loving arms around our weary bodies. He infuses us with great strength and determination to go where He has called us. Let us spring into action by following *God* to the places where He needs us. We will find our *God* given purpose when we seek Him and the desires He has for us first and foremost. The desires of our own heart will become His desires when we draw closer to His love.

The closer to love we get, the more joy we will find. More of His love equals more of His joy. As we give our whole hearts to *God*, our joy multiplies! Let us find that joy and sing songs of praise and thanksgiving to our *Lord* and *Savior* forevermore!

Hold Fast to Him in Love and Let Him Deliver You

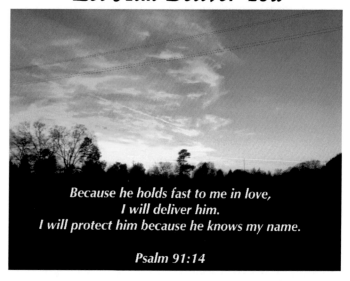

Because he holds fast to me in love,
I will deliver him.
I will protect him because he knows my name.

Psalm 91:14

Because you hold fast to Him in love, He will deliver you. He will protect you, because you know his name. The *Lord* is your protector and your deliverer. He is your defender. His mighty power will be with you as you draw to Him and believe. The same power that raised *Jesus* from the dead lives in you. The same *Spirit* that lives in Him lives in you. Activate this power and *Spirit* by drawing closer to *Jesus*, the giver of life!

He loves you so much and wants you to be closer to Him. Love Him and let Him guide you. He holds you up with His right hand. He will never let go of you, so why are you afraid? Let your faith be bigger and your fear will disappear. Get your strength from the one who always strengthens you. Only *Jesus* and His word of life will take you to that place of hope again. Let His words of life settle in your soul and your heart. His words are the sword of the *Spirit* and will prepare you for the battle.

Call to your *Lord*, and He will deliver you. Keep praying and believing! Yield to the *Holy Spirit* and be filled with the power that comes from Him. Find your peace in *Jesus* as you let Him rule in your heart. Your soul will be filled with unspeakable joy as you settle in closer to the love of *Jesus*. Find your joy in *Jesus Christ*!

Today if You Hear His Voice, do not Harden Your Heart

For He is our God,
and we are the people of His pasture,
and the sheep of his hand.
Today , if you hear His voice,
do not harden your hearts.

Psalm 95:7-8

For He is our *God*, and we are the people of His pasture, and the sheep of His hand. Today, if you hear His voice, do not harden your hearts. He is calling you to come to Him. Do you hear your Good Shepherd? Will you come into His sheepfold so that He can restore you? Will you open your heart to His love and His glory?

You are His beloved sheep, and He wants to protect you. He desires to bring you into His pasture where you will find comfort and rest. He desires good for you. He loves you and wants your heart. Open you heart so that He can soften it. Do not harden your heart but open your heart wide! Let the *Lord* restore the joy of your salvation. Let Him lead you into His still pastures where you will find comfort and rest. There you will find peace. There you will feel the love of your *Savior*. Let His love surround you. Open your arms to the love that is waiting for you through your *Lord Jesus*!

The victory has been won for you. *Jesus* has overcome the world for you. Do you believe that He loves you? If you truly believe, you will be made new. Your heart will be fully transformed by the love of *Jesus*, maybe for the first time in your life. When you come back to Him, *Jesus* will restore the joy of your salvation to your soul and your spirit! Come back to *Jesus*! He wants to revive, restore and rebuild you!

Whoever Keeps His Mouth and His Tongue Keeps Himself Out of Trouble

Whoever keeps his mouth and his tongue keeps himself out of trouble. The *Lord* desires for us to use our words wisely. He needs us to build others up with our words and not tear them down. When we give our tongues to Him, the *Lord* can use us more fully for His greater good. We can be examples of truth and righteousness when we trust Him to direct our speech and conduct. It is our choice how we respond to *God's* calling. He needs us to follow Him faithfully by saying yes. He wants us to find Him. He needs us to be willing to be used for His greater purpose and glory.

His desire is for our greater good. He can use us to edify and encourage those who need hope. Many need an encouraging word or positive influence in their life. Let us host the presence of *God* and let His sweetness and gentleness of *Spirit* reside in us. As we let the *Holy Spirit* lead us to sow seeds of kindness and love, we will smell the sweet aroma of the blossoms that will begin to grow abundantly around us. When the *Lord* is in control, our tongue and mouth will begin to bless and not curse others. Our acts of kindness will flow from a giving heart turned towards the *Lord*. We could be that one person who could change a heart towards *God* by our speech and our actions. Let us be the blessing that brings hope and peace to a lost and troubled world! The *Lord* needs us now!

Blessed are the Eyes that See What You See

Blessed are the eyes that see what you see.

Luke 10:23

Finding Joy in Jesus

Blessed are the eyes that see what you see. You will see *Jesus* all around you when you are following Him. He shows himself to those who follow Him faithfully. He blesses those who love Him by trusting Him and obeying His commandments. Look to *Jesus*, the author and perfecter of your faith. He needs you to be present with Him. He cherishes you, His beloved! Give *Jesus* your whole heart. You will see what He wants you to see when you are fully connected to Him by faith.

Your sadness will become your greatest joy with *Jesus* by your side. Your heart will be filled with gladness and hope. Your soul will be full of peace beyond understanding. Your eyes will see with compassion and mercy. With His eyes, you will want to be all that *Jesus* needs you to be. Open the eyes of your heart to see *Jesus*. Follow Him to places He wants to take you. Trust Him to guide you always. His way is the only way to find life. Let His love cover you completely. Let His hope comfort you and hold you up. Let His joy fill you so that you will sparkle and shine!

Blessed Rather are Those Who Hear the Word of God and Keep it!

Blessed rather are those who hear the word of God and keep it!

Luke 11:28

Blessed rather are those who hear the word of *God* and keep it! *God* blesses those who listen and obey His words of truth. We hear Him by reading His word and opening our hearts to His truth for us. He wants to direct our paths and needs us to be open to hear Him. Follow the *Lord* so that you will have life. Make Him the *Lord* of your life by trusting His way. There are many ways to live, but only His way is the way that leads to life.

Blessed are you when you stay on the path that the *Lord* has prepared for you. It is your choice to live a joy-filled life with *Jesus*. Choose joy with *Jesus*! Say yes to the blessings waiting for you. Open your heart to the love that is yours through *Jesus Christ*. Keep the word of the *Lord* close to your heart and stay connected to Him by praying consistently. Faithfully follow where He leads you. He will bless you and keep you when you make Him the *Lord* of your life. The joy of the *Lord* will be your strength and your song all the day long. Every day will be a good day when you get real with the *Lord* by keeping Him close to your heart, soul, and spirit. Keep Him close and be filled with His power and love!

For Whoever Finds the Lord Finds Life and Obtains Favor from the Lord

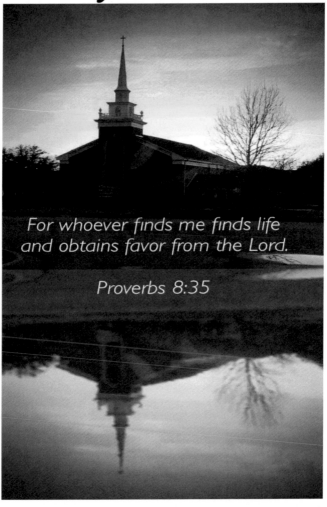

For whoever finds me finds life and obtains favor from the Lord.

Proverbs 8:35

For whoever finds the *Lord*, finds life and obtains favor from the *Lord*. When you seek Him with all of your heart, you will find Him. The *Lord* will give you even more than you can ever ask or imagine. Find *Jesus* and love Him with all of your heart. Let His love cover you with more joy. He loves you so much and will give you all of His love if you will take it. More of His love equals more of His joy. Every moment spent with the *Lord* will give you more of these great opportunities for more joy!

Do not miss a single day with the *Lord* by your side. Hold Him close in your heart. Let Him comfort you and rescue you from your heartache and pain. Only He can take your struggles and turn them into joy. Believe that the joy of the *Lord* is your strength. Ask Him for more! He wants to give you more of His love so that you can have more life. He favors those who love Him and follow Him. If you love the *Lord* your *God* with all your heart, soul, and strength, you will surrender all to Him. Surrendering all to the *Lord* will give you peace and comfort. Your faith will grow through the places where there was once pain. With the *Lord* in control, your greatest fear will become your greatest triumph! Where you are weak, He is strong for you. He will take your weaknesses and use it all for His glory! Let the *Lord* shine His blessings and glory upon you today! Today is the day that the *Lord* has made for you, so rejoice and be glad in it!

By Your Endurance You Will Gain Your Lives

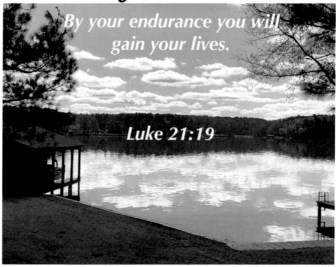

By your endurance you will gain your lives.

Luke 21:19

By your endurance you will gain your lives. Keep on believing and keep on persevering with *Jesus*. You will be filled with life when you keep running the race that is marked for you by *Jesus*. He needs you to keep on the path He has made for you with endurance. He will give you the strength you need to finish. There are many ways to go, but only one way that leads to life through *Jesus Christ*. Seek Him and you will find that route of hope. There is peace along the path after the storm. You may enter this route with *Jesus* any time you choose to believe and run your race. He wants you to keep on going to find freedom and new life. Smooth places exist as well as bumps along this windy and narrow road. Follow His light of hope and find the joy of renewed life that is waiting for you along this lighted path.

There is much to gain when you trust the *Lord* above yourself. He is the one who will direct you and challenge you to greater hope, peace, and joy. Your life will be fuller, and your future will be brighter with *Jesus*. Beauty still does exist through the ashes of life. Only through *Jesus* will you find this beautiful life. Keep fighting the good fight of faith and discover that your endurance will be rewarded. The crown of life is yours when you are running the race marked for you with *Jesus Christ*! Go run it and live your life well!

Many are the Plans in the Mind of a Man, but it is the Purpose of the Lord that Prevails

Many are the plans in the mind of a man, but it is the purpose of the Lord that will stand.

Proverbs 19:21

Many are the plans in the mind of a man, but it is the purpose of the *Lord* that will stand. The *Lord* has a plan and a purpose that is greater than anything we can ever dream or imagine. He desires for us to find our *God* given purpose as we seek more of Him. Let us begin anew and find His desire for our lives. He has good planned for us, so let us walk in it. We will find new life with *Jesus* when we put Him in the center of it and truly follow Him and His will for our lives. Let us make the most of the life that He wants to give us. Let us run with endurance the race He has given us. Let us not stop believing that His plans for us are far better. Let us lay aside every weight that hinders us and turn towards *Jesus*. He will take all of our pain and give us peace.

He needs us to be willing to follow Him by simply trusting and obeying Him. He will show us the way to go. He will be our peace in the midst of any storm that comes our way. He is our hope when there is pain and suffering around us. He is that bright light. Find the light of hope and be filled with the power of the *Holy Spirit* through *Jesus Christ* our *Lord*. Take the peace that only He gives and know that He is enough!

Let Your Hearts Not Be Troubled

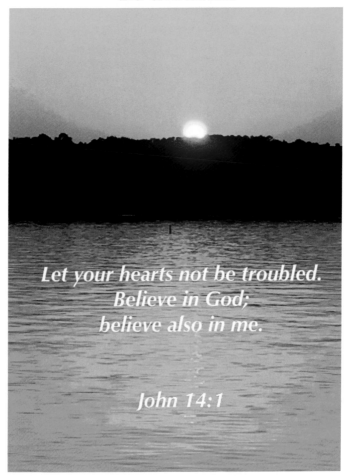

Let your hearts not be troubled.
Believe in God;
believe also in me.

John 14:1

"Let your hearts not be troubled. Believe in *God*, believe also in me." These words of *Jesus* are so comforting and true. If we believe in *God* the *Father* and His *Son, Jesus*, we will have life. He has come to give us life through His life. We can now know and have a relationship with *God* through *Jesus Christ*, His *Son*. His grace is sufficient for us! He came to free us from our sins, so we can live an abundant life in *Christ*. Why are we troubled? Why do we not have peace? Why do we not believe? Why are we living in fear instead of fearing the *Lord*?

Let us lay aside our troubles, anxieties, worries, and fears and start trusting our *Savior* by giving more of ourselves to *Jesus*. Today is the day to start really living for *Jesus*. There is nothing we can do to make *Jesus* love us more, and there is nothing we can do to make Him love us less. He loves us right where we are. He just needs us to accept His love by trusting Him. His grace is enough. Let us love Him and live victoriously in *Christ*. He has made us whole again. He has washed away our sins through His death and sacrifice on the cross. Let us come back to *Jesus* and find peace again. He is our peace. He will light up our life!

Praise the Lord as Long as You Live, Sing Praises to God as Long as You Have Being

I praise the Lord as long as I live;
I will sing praises to my God while I have my being.

Psalm 146:2

We will praise the *Lord* as long as we live, we will sing praises to our *God* as long as we have our being. We have so much to be thankful for as we have been given the greatest gift, our *Lord, Jesus Christ*! He has come to bless us with new life and give us new hope! We are made new, because we have a *Savior* who has taken all of our sins and shame. He has put a new song in our heart, and we will rejoice and sing praises to Him! Let us live with this renewed hope and life once again. Let us love with the love that *Jesus* has given us. Let us encourage one another as He has encouraged us. Let us continually give Him all the glory and praise for what He is doing in us and through us!

We are stronger in *Christ*. He uses our weaknesses for His glory. When we are weak, He becomes our strength. He uses every part of us that He needs to accomplish His purposes on earth. Let us be faithful and obedient to His calling. He needs us to be His hands and feet as long as we have being. *Jesus* knows our hearts. He sees our desires and yearns for us to desire Him first. Make Him your first love, and see Him work wonders and miracles as He blesses those who faithfully follow Him! Let us open our eyes to His glory now and forevermore!

Be Merciful, Even as Your Father is Merciful

Be merciful,
even as your Father is merciful.

John 6:36

Be merciful, even as your *Father* is merciful. He is forgiving with you, so forgive others. The measure of compassion and forgiveness you have for others will be given to you by your *Father* in heaven. His Son, *Jesus*, has left the grave so that you can leave your past behind. He has forgiven all of your past sins so that you can be free at last! He gives you hope through His mercy and grace. He gives you new life through His promise to never abandon you. Cling to *Jesus* and discover that His love will endure forever.

His compassion for you is real! His grace is all you need. Give the grace that you have been given. Be the one to forgive others first, because of the sacrifice that *Christ* made first for you! You will experience true freedom as you forgive! You will find it all when you give it all. He paid it all so that you can have a close relationship with His *Father*. *God* loves you so much. He has great compassion for you. He cares for you so deeply. Believe that you have been forgiven. Find joy knowing that you can have life again through His Son, *Jesus*! Receive the great gift of grace by choosing to follow *Jesus Christ*!

Behold the Virgin Shall Conceive and Bear a Son

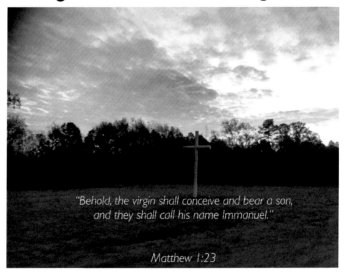

"Behold, the virgin shall conceive and bear a son, and they shall call his name Immanuel."

Matthew 1:23

"Behold, the virgin shall conceive and bear a son, and they shall call Him Immanuel." The angel of the *Lord* spoke to Joseph and told him this glorious news! He told him not to be afraid but to expect a miracle in the birth of this baby who would be the *Savior* of the world! He would be *God* with us, our *Savior, Jesus*, who would come to save us from our sins! Can you imagine hearing this from an angel of the *Lord*? Can you just feel the excitement, fear, and anticipation that Joseph must have felt? His wife, Mary would conceive from the *Holy Spirit,* a child who would be our *Savior*! This was unbelievable, but He believed. Do you believe that you have a *Savior* in *Jesus*? Do you know that *God* loved you so much that He gave you the greatest gift? The best gift that you have and ever will receive is wrapped in swaddling clothes!

Have you unwrapped your gift of *Jesus*? Have you experienced the true and complete love of your *Savior*? This Christmas season can be the most special and meaningful if you just unwrap and receive *Jesus*, the greatest gift that you have ever been given. *God* gave you this most wonderful gift! Do not be afraid and do not fear for *Jesus* is here for you today! Everyday can be filled with His presence if you choose to host Him in your life! Open your gift of *Jesus* and be filled with hope, peace, and joy!

When They Saw the Star, They Rejoiced Exceedingly with Great Joy

When they saw the star,
they rejoiced exceedingly with great joy.

Matthew 2:10

When they saw the star, they rejoiced exceedingly with great joy. The promise of a new life through a *Savior* was seen in that bright star. All glory to *God* in the highest for bringing us a *Savior*! *Jesus Christ* would save us from our sins! He would be the light of the world! He would be love! And He would be our *Lord*! All who believed in Him would be saved. All who chose to love Him would be free at last. *God* gave us His *Son* so that we could experience a freedom and a hope.

Many were waiting for the *Messiah*. The birth of *Jesus* brought the good news far and wide. The light from the star brought hope. The excitement and wonder was real for the people then and it is real for us today. *Jesus* is real in our lives when we get real with Him. He wants to be our *Lord* and *Savior* and needs us to give Him our whole heart. When we give Him our whole heart, we can experience peace beyond understanding and joy beyond measure! Our hope is found in our *Lord Jesus*. See the light of the *Savior* of the world, feel the warmth of His everlasting love, and know that He is *Lord* of all. Peace on earth and goodwill to all men is found through the greatest gift, *Jesus Christ*! All glory to *God* in the highest!

Let all God's Angels Rejoice Him

And again, when he brings the firstborn
into the world he says,
"Let all God's angels worship him."

Hebrews 1:6

And again, when He brings the firstborn into the world He says, "Let all *God's* angels worship Him." Let all rejoice, for a king will be born who will bring glory to all! Let heaven and earth rejoice as the *Savior* will be great among men and rule over all! He will bring peace on earth and goodwill to all men. He will bring joy to the whole world! Let us magnify our *Lord* and *Savior*, *Jesus Christ*! Let us rejoice, for He has been born to take away our sins. This little baby will be the great I Am, a holy child given to us from our *God*, our *Father. Emmanuel* will be with us always.

We will be able to see unspeakable joy everywhere around us when we see with new eyes. Let us open the eyes of our heart to experience the love of our *Savior*. Let us celebrate His birth with a new joy as we draw closer in our spirit to Him. Let us seek more of *Jesus* and His *Spirit*! Let us worship Him like the angels around and among us. Let us be an angel on earth as we give the love of *Jesus* to others. Let us love with the heart of *Jesus* as He loves us so deeply! Let us rejoice together, for a *Savior* is born and there is joy when we find *Jesus*! That joy is waiting for us, so what are we waiting for?

Find Life in Him as He is Life and the Light of Men

In Him was life,
and the life was the light of men

John 1:4

In Him was life, and the life was the light of men. *Jesus Christ* was born to give us life. Our worn-out bodies and weary souls need *Jesus*! He brings life to light up the darkness. He brings hope to our hearts once again. His birth and resurrection are proof of His great love for us. He came as a man to live among us in this troubled and sin-filled world. He who was without sin, died for ours so that we could have life. His resurrection has given us new life. Let us choose to take it.

Find the miracle of Christmas and the promise of new life in *Jesus*. He is waiting for us to come to Him and to trust Him with our whole heart. Be still in His presence and discover the pure joy that only *Jesus* can give. Let Him fill our longing souls and soften our hardened hearts with His joy! The joy of *Jesus* is real! We can have this joy when we choose *Jesus* over ourselves. In Him is the light of men. Come to the light and discover everlasting and great joy!

Believe that God so Loved the World that He Gave His Only Son to You

For God so loved the world
that he gave his only Son,
that whoever believes in him
should not perish but have eternal life.

John 3:16

"For *God* so loved the world that He gave His only *Son*, that whoever believes in Him should not perish but have eternal life." Yes, *God* loved you then and He loves you now. Worship Him like the shepherds and the wise men did that night when the *Savior* was born! They saw the bright light and followed the star to the place where they saw their *Savior* and experienced the wonder of His birth! Look for the love of *Jesus* with fresh eyes. Feel His love for you that He gives freely. Wrap yourself up in His amazing grace. Take all that He gives to you. He wants to give you everything your heart desires. More hope, peace, joy, and love are yours, if you just believe.

Out of His love, *God* has given you freedom to love Him. Take all that is yours in *Christ* and let Him welcome you into the family of *God*. Only through the love of *Christ* can you have a relationship with the *Father*. *Jesus Christ* was born to give you a direct connection to His *Father*. You can only get to the *Father* through His *Son*. Believe in Him so that you can have everlasting life. Your gift is ready for you to unwrap and receive. You can and will experience the joy of Christmas if you open and receive the most glorious gift that is found wrapped in swaddling clothes just for you. You will find joy as you take and receive your gift of *Jesus*! Joy to the world, the *Lord* has come! Let earth receive her *King*! Let every heart prepare Him room, and heaven and nature will sing!

Commit Your Work to the Lord and Your Plans Will Succeed

Commit your work to the Lord
and your plans will be established.

Proverbs 16:3

      Commit your work to the *Lord* and your plans will be established. Love Him with all of your heart. Give Him the first fruits of your life and the best portion will be yours. Your dreams and desires can come true when your heart is in the right place. Serve and honor *God* and see how your life will be blessed. You have been chosen by the *Lord* and He has plans for you to succeed. The *Lord* has a future and a hope for you. Do you believe this? Do you want all that has been planned for you? Are you walking by faith by choosing to follow *Jesus*? Are you ready to receive all that is yours in *Christ Jesus*? If so, open your heart completely to the *Lord Jesus*. Trust Him with your whole heart. Surrender your fears, insecurities, anxieties, and worries to Him. Tell Him your dreams and desires as you pray. Open your ears to what He is telling you as you read His words of truth. You can hear His voice if you do not harden your heart.

Once you hear Him, open your eyes to see what He needs you to do. The eyes of your heart will be enlightened as you surrender all to *Jesus*. Follow Him by opening the eyes of your heart to discover the gifts He has for you. He wants to create a new spirit of joy in you! You will be amazed at all He wants to give you. Open your arms to receive what the *Lord* has for you. As you love the *Lord* with your arms wide open and abide in His love, you will be able to love others unconditionally. As you love, you will feel love. Commit your plans, your heart, your mind, and your soul to the *Lord*. Then, dream big and pray bigger because blessings are waiting for you if you believe!

About the Author

Jill Lowry is an ardent follower of Jesus who has a desire and passion to communicate His truth. Her writings combine the accuracy of a scholar with the practicality of a wife and mother. Jill grew up in San Antonio, Texas. She graduated from the University of Texas with a Bachelor of Business Administration in Marketing and holds a law degree from St. Mary's University in San Antonio. She resides in northeast Texas with her husband and two children.

Her ministries include helping mentor and feed at-risk students, co-leading a women's bible study, co-hosting a weekly radio show that answers questions of faith, and praying with fellow believers in a weekly community prayer group.

Jill is the founder and president of a student mentoring and food program, Mt. Vernon Cares, created for at-risk students at the local Junior High and High School. She is also one of the hosts of a faith-based weekly radio talk show, Real Life Real People.

Jill takes every opportunity to pray with friends and neighbors in need and considers intercessory prayer a vital part of her ministry.

She is part of a weekly community prayer group which meets on the Downtown Square to pray for revival in her community and beyond.

This is her first book. Her desire is that you will be encouraged to find your joy in Jesus through her photographs, applications of scripture, and truth from the Holy Spirit found in this book.

.

Prayers and Praises

A personal journal

Prayers and Praises

A personal journal

Prayers and Praises

A personal journal

Prayers and Praises

A personal journal

Prayers and Praises

A personal journal

Prayers and Praises

A personal journal

Prayers and Praises

A personal journal

Made in the USA
San Bernardino, CA
10 February 2018